GUITAR CHORDS/LYRICS

# BRANDI CARLILE

## THE FIREWATCHER'S DAUGHTER

ISBN 978-1-4950-1412-3

**HAL•LEONARD®**

Visit Hal Leonard Online at
**www.halleonard.com**

Contact us:
**Hal Leonard**
7777 West Bluemound Road
Milwaukee, WI 53213
Email: info@halleonard.com

In Europe, contact:
**Hal Leonard Europe Limited**
42 Wigmore Street
Marylebone, London, W1U 2RN
Email: info@halleonardeurope.com

In Australia, contact:
**Hal Leonard Australia Pty. Ltd.**
4 Lentara Court
Cheltenham, Victoria, 3192 Australia
Email: info@halleonard.com.au

# Wherever Is Your Heart

**Words and Music by Tim Hanseroth and Brandi Carlile**

*Recording sounds one step higher than written due to capo.

_____ may take _____ you far _____ from me, I know _____

wher - ev - er is _____ your heart _____ I _____ call _____

_____ home. _____

**Verse**

made me feel _____ like I _____ was al - ways fall - ing. _____ Al - ways fall -

- ing down _____ with - out a place _____ to land. _____

Some - where in _____ the dis - tance, heard you call - ing. _____ It hurt _____

_____ so bad _____ to let go of your hand. _____ Wher -

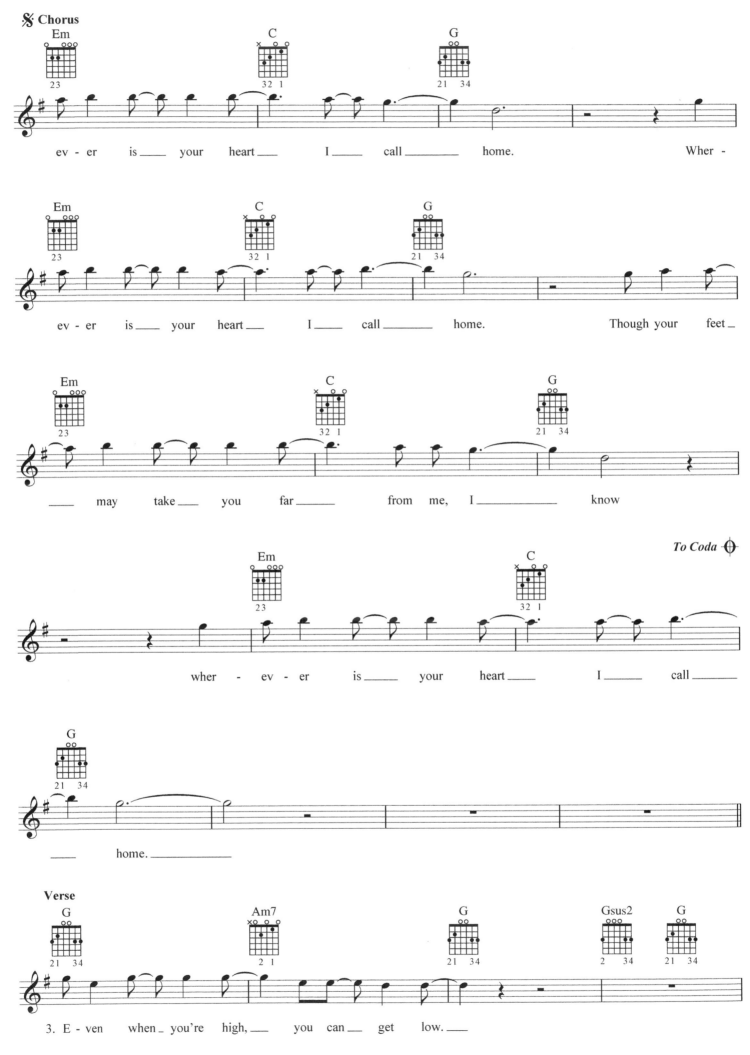

E - ven with \_ the friends \_\_\_ you love, \_ you're still a - lone. We

al - ways find \_\_\_ the dark - est place to go. \_\_\_\_

God for - give \_\_\_ our minds, \_\_\_ we were

*D.S. al Coda*

N.C.

born to roam. _____ Wher -

**⊕ Coda**

\_\_\_\_ home. _____

God \_

**Bridge**

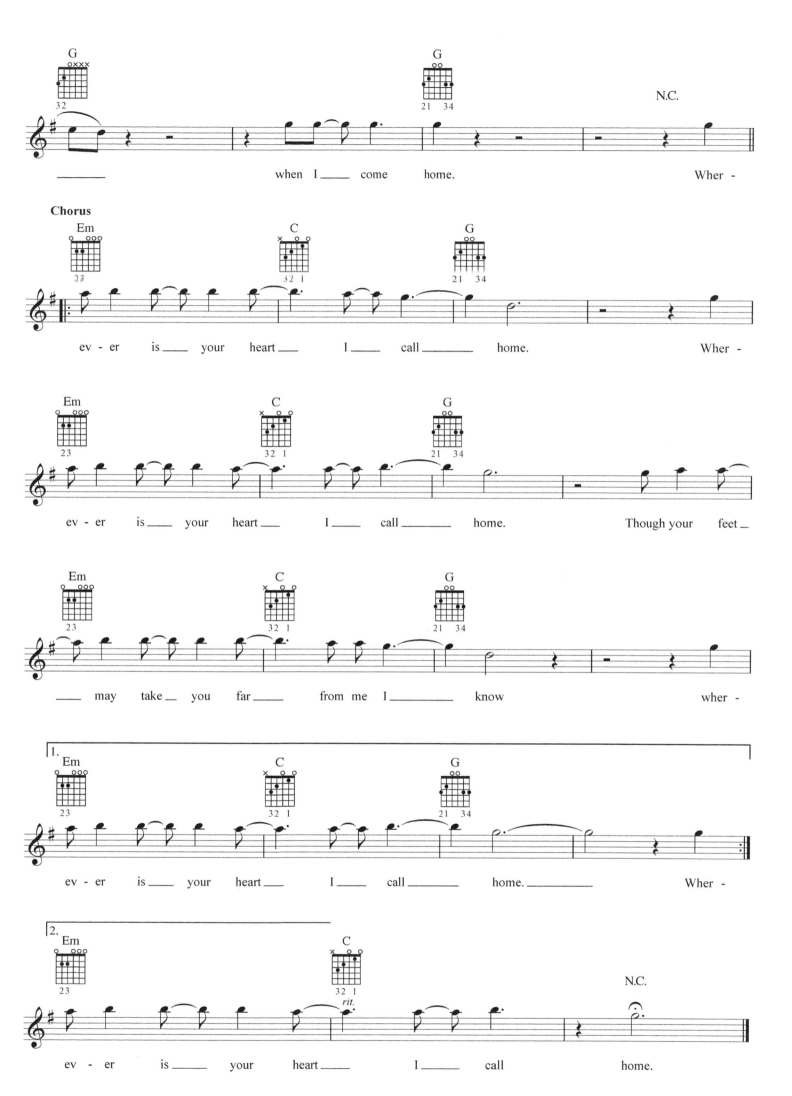

when I ____ come home. Wher -

**Chorus**

ev - er is ____ your heart ____ I ____ call ____ home. Wher -

ev - er is ____ your heart ____ I ____ call ____ home. Though your feet ___

____ may take ___ you far ____ from me I ____ know wher -

1.

ev - er is ____ your heart ____ I ____ call ____ home. ____ Wher -

2.

ev - er is ____ your heart ____ I ____ call home.

# The Eye

**Words and Music by Tim Hanseroth and Brandi Carlile**

Capo VI

**Intro**

Moderately slow, in 2  ♩ = 78

*Recording sounds 3 steps higher than written due to capo.
**T = thumb

**Verse**

1. It real - ly breaks my heart _____ to see a dear old _ friend
2. Where did you learn to walk? _____ Where did you learn to _ run

go down _ to the worn _ out place _ a - gain. _
a - way _ from ev - 'ry - thing _____ you love? _

Do you know the sound _____ of a clos - ing _ door?
Did you think the bot - tle would ev - er ease your _ pain?

Have you heard that sound some - where be - fore? \_\_\_\_ Do you
Did you think \_\_ that love's \_\_ a fool - ish game? _____ Did you

won - der if \_\_ she knows \_\_ you an - y - more? _____
find some - one \_\_ else \_\_\_\_ to take \_ the blame? _____
I

**Chorus**

wrapped your love a - round \_\_ me like a chain, \_\_ but I

nev - er was a - fraid _____ that it would die. _____

You can dance \_\_ in a hur - ri - cane _____ but

on - ly if \_\_\_\_ you're stand - ing in \_\_\_\_ the eye. _____

1.

2.

You can dance ___ in a hur - ri - cane ___ but on - ly if ___ you're stand - ing in ___ the eye. ___

**Interlude**

**Verse**

3. I am a stur - dy soul. _____ And there ain't no ___ shame in ly - ing down ___ in the bed ___ you made. ___ Can you fight the urge ___ to run ___ for an - oth - er day? _____

# The Things I Regret

**Words and Music by Tim Hanseroth,
Brandi Carlile and Phil Hanseroth**

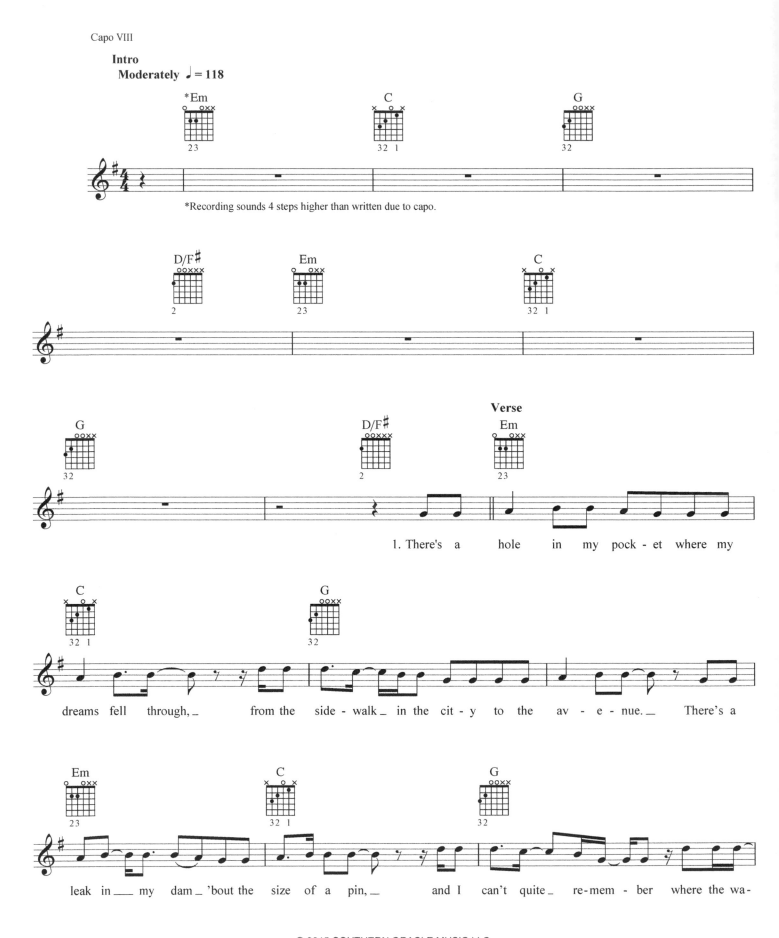

*Recording sounds 4 steps higher than written due to capo.

1. There's a hole in my pock-et where my dreams fell through, ___ from the side-walk ___ in the cit-y to the av-e-nue. ___ There's a leak in ___ my dam ___ 'bout the size of a pin, ___ and I can't quite ___ re-mem-ber where the wa-

**Verse**

weight of __ the world __ rest-ing on my __ back __ and the road in which __ I've trav-eled is as long __ __ as it's __ cracked. I keep __ press - ing for-ward with my feet to the __ ground, for a heart __ __ that is bro - ken makes a beau-ti-ful sound. __ When you're wear-ing on __ your sleeve __ all the things __ __ you re-gret, you can on - ly __ re - mem - ber what you want to __ for - get. __

**Chorus**

__ Let them roll __ o - ver me. Let them roll __ o - ver me when I doubt __ __ you, __ Let them roll __ o - ver me. Let them roll __ o - ver me __ when I doubt __ you. __

Interlude

Verse

walk through my days like a ghost in a dream, but the feel car - ries on, and my

past fol-lows me. It's hard mov - ing on from the things you've done wrong when they

play in your head like an old fash - ioned song. When you're wear-ing on your sleeve all the things

you re-gret, you can on - ly re-mem-ber what you want to for-get. Lone - ly

15

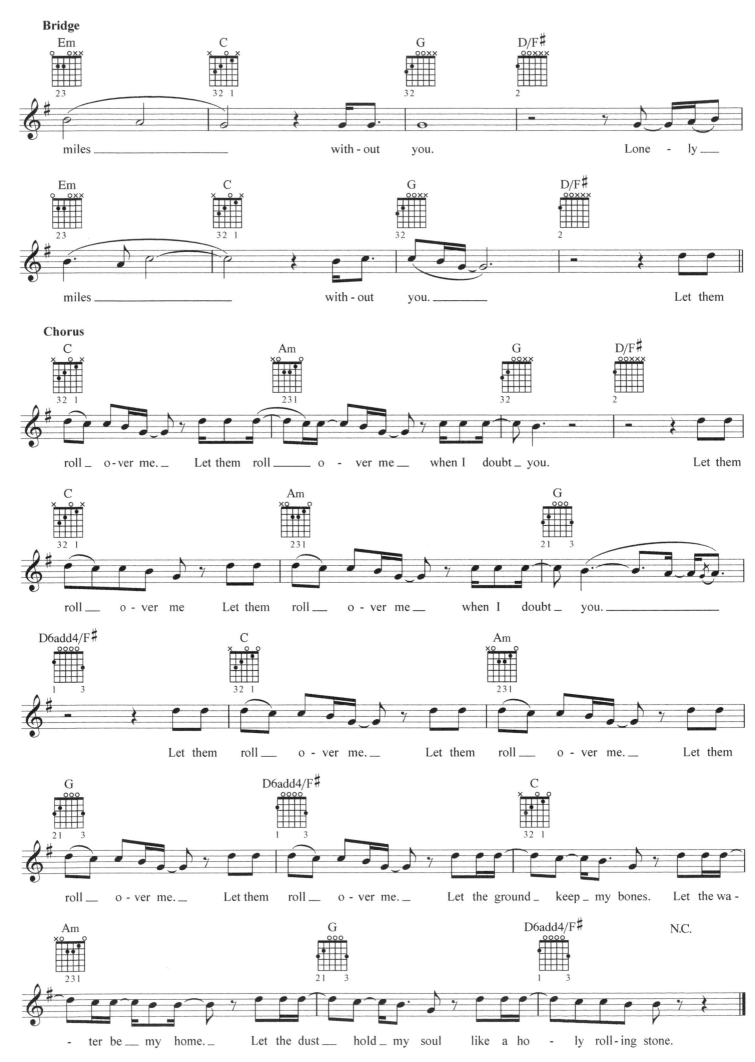

# Mainstream Kid

**Words and Music by Brandi Carlile and Tim Hanseroth**

You can own me, you con-trol___ me. In-di-vid-u-al-i-ty has

never stood a chance a-gainst_ you. Jump in-to the main - stream.

2. Your rev-o-   Jump in-to the main - stream.

**Interlude**

N.C.(A)

*Play 3 times*

G

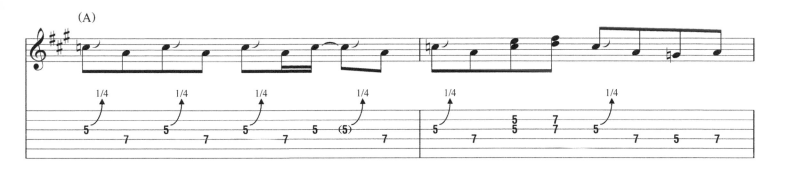

**Interlude**

N.C.(A)

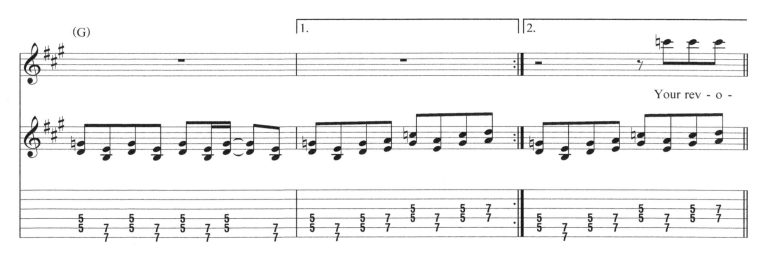

Your rev - o -

**Outro**

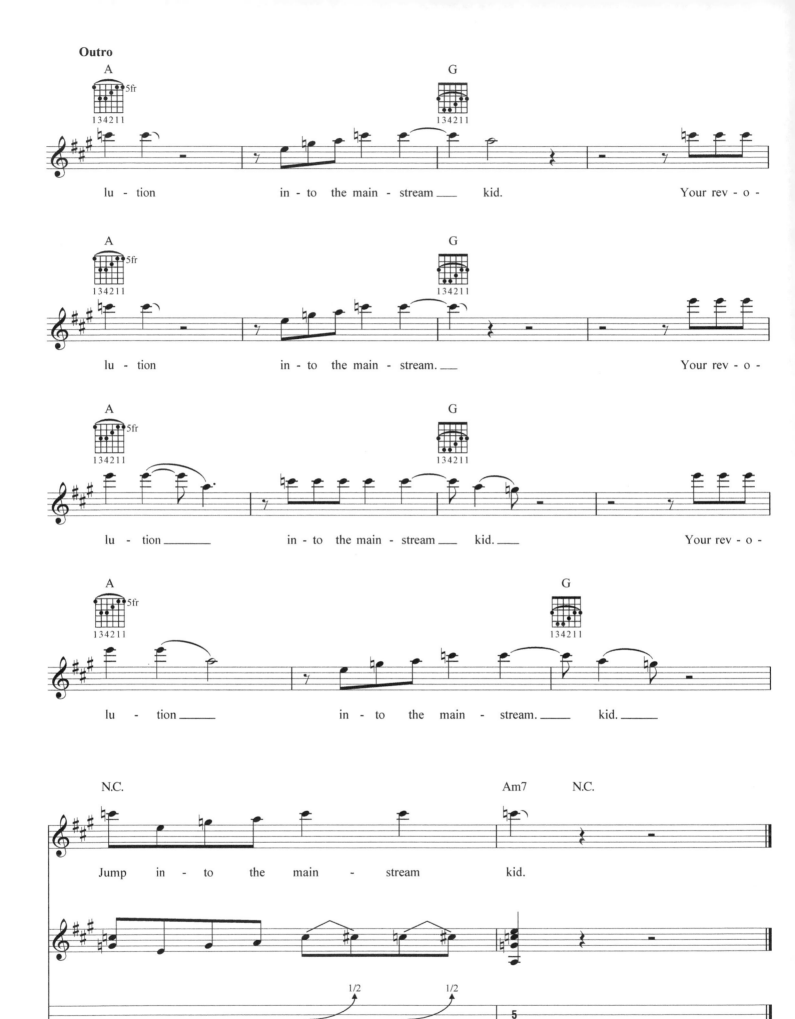

# Beginning To Feel The Years

**Words and Music by Phil Hanseroth**

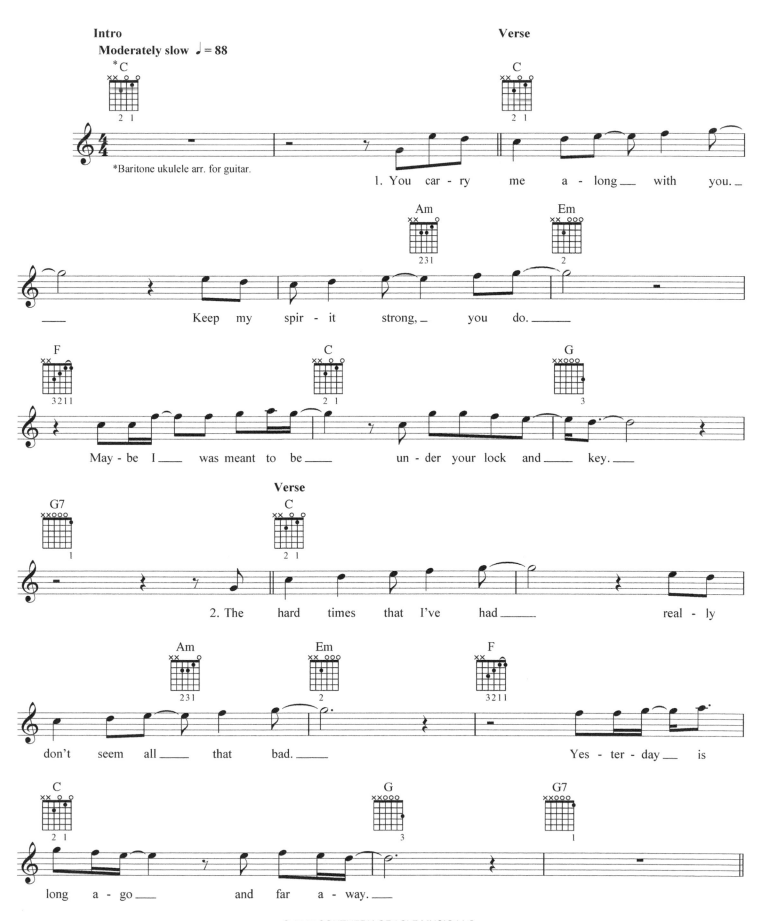

**𝄋 Chorus**

I'm be-gin-ning to feel the years, ___ but I'm go-ing to be o-
And I'm be-gin-ning to feel the years, ___

kay as long as you're ___ be - side _____ me a - long ___ the way. ___

___ I'm gon-na make it through ___ the night ___ and in-to morn - ing

*To Coda* ⊕ **Interlude**

light. _____

**Verse**

3. There are things I said be - fore, ___ I don't

mean them an - y - more. ___ Yes - ter - day ___ is

**D.S. al Coda**

long a - go ___ and far a - way. ___

# Wilder (We're Chained)

**Words and Music by Tim Hanseroth**

With a heart so heav - y \_\_\_\_ and beat - ing like \_\_\_ a drum, \_\_

nei - ther did \_\_\_ you look \_\_\_\_ like \_\_\_ your \_\_

grand - fa - ther's son. \_\_\_\_\_ We're

### 𝄋 Chorus

chained, _____ and when

ev - 'ry - thing \_ else chang - es \_\_\_\_ our love will stay \_ the same. \_\_\_ We're

chained, _____ and when

ev - 'ry - thing___ else   goes  a - way___ our   love   will  still___ re - main.___

___   We're  chained. ___

*To Coda 2*   *To Coda 1*

**Verse**

2. Wild - er  than ___ a   brush ___ fi - re ___ burns   deep   in - side ___ the  bram -

ble,              ba - by,  I ___ think ___ God ___ made ___ your

soul   born ___ to  ram - ble.

May - be  you'll  take ___ to ___ the   far   a - way ___ plac -

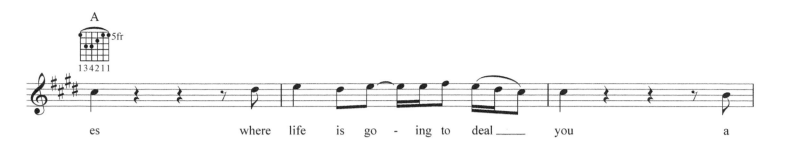

es where life is go - ing to deal _____ you a

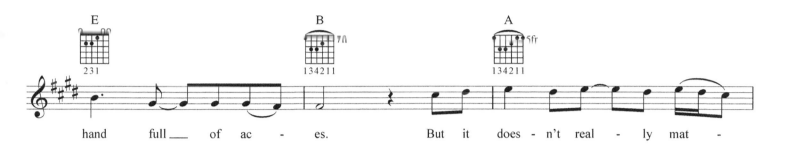

hand full _ of ac - es. But it does - n't real - ly mat -

*D.S. al Coda 1*

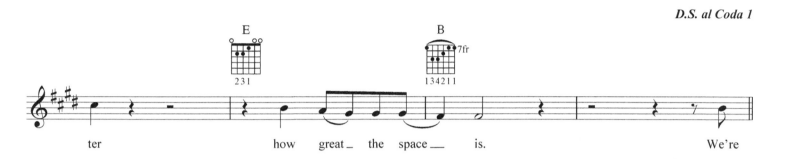

ter how great _ the space _ is. We're

**⊕ Coda 1**

**Verse**

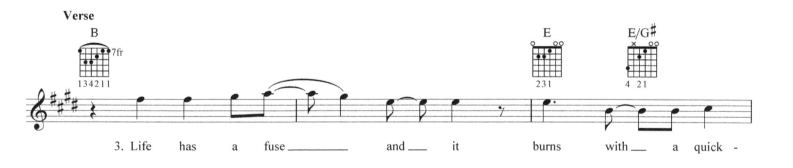

3. Life has a fuse _____ and _ it burns with _ a quick -

ness, but death ain't _ the long _____ twist - ed

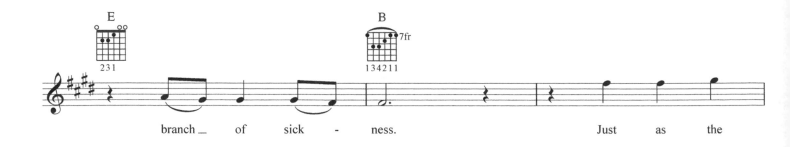

branch __ of sick - ness. Just as the

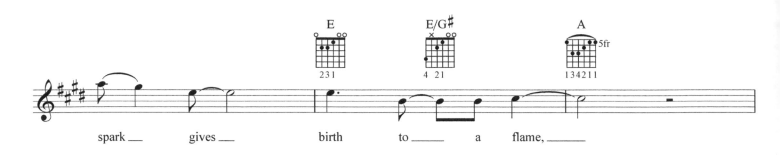

spark __ gives __ birth to __ a flame, _____

we'll be bound __ by ____ our love _____ and __

*D.S. al Coda 2*

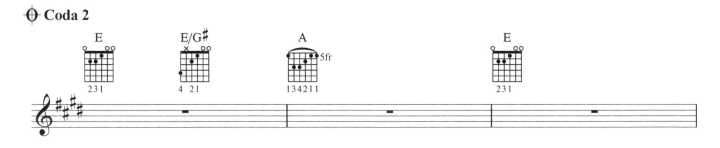

in ___ the fam - 'ly name. _____ We're

⊕ **Coda 2**

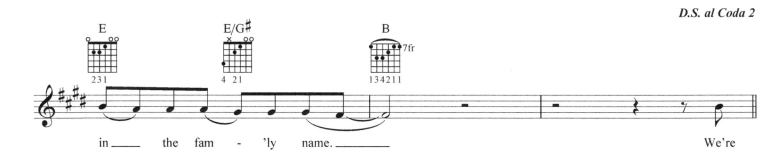

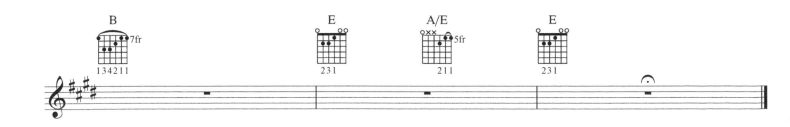

# Blood Muscle Skin & Bone

**Words and Music by Phil Hanseroth**

Drop D tuning, down 1/2 step:
(low to high) Db-Ab-Db-Gb-Bb-Eb

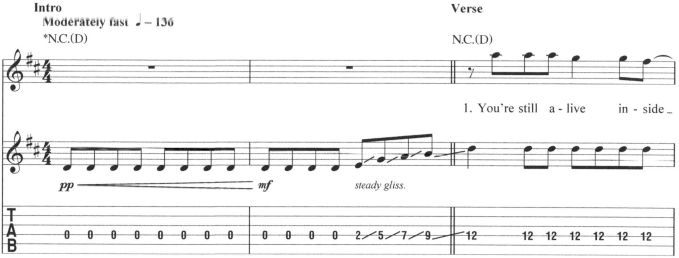

*Recording sounds a half step lower than written due to tuning.

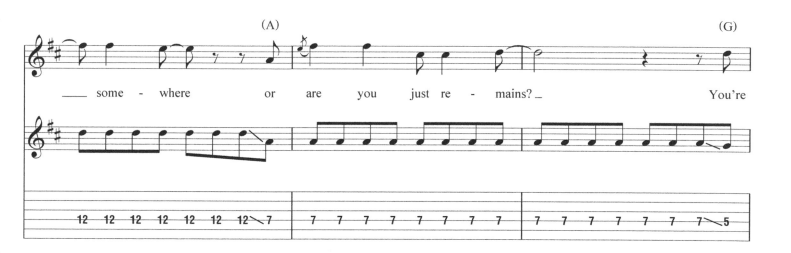

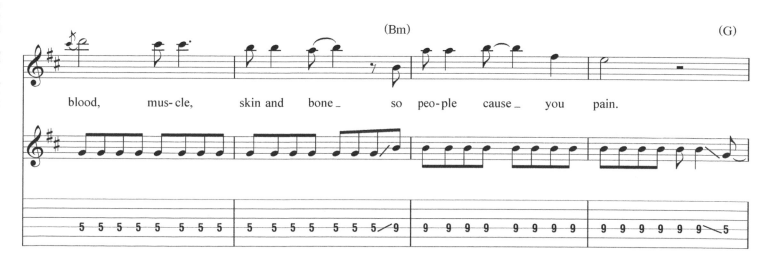

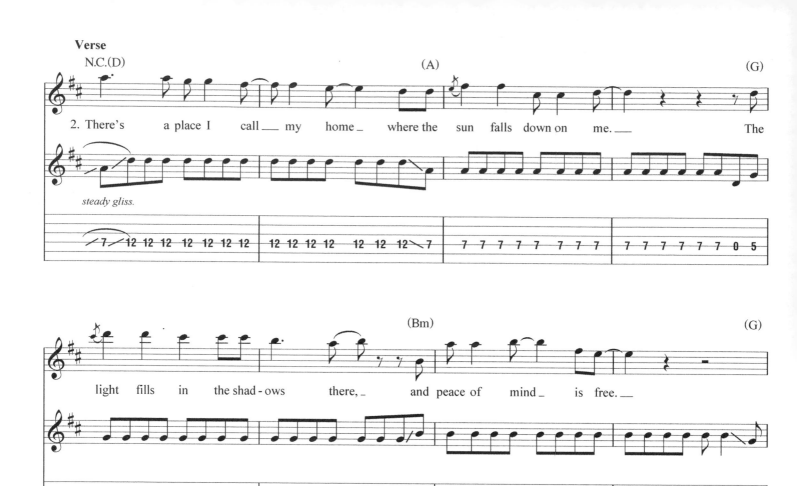

2. There's a place I call my home where the sun falls down on me. The

*steady gliss.*

light fills in the shad-ows there, and peace of mind is free.

But far be-low that place a tear forms in my eye.

*D.S. al Coda*

The shad-ows have no foe there, and dark-ness mul - ti-plies.

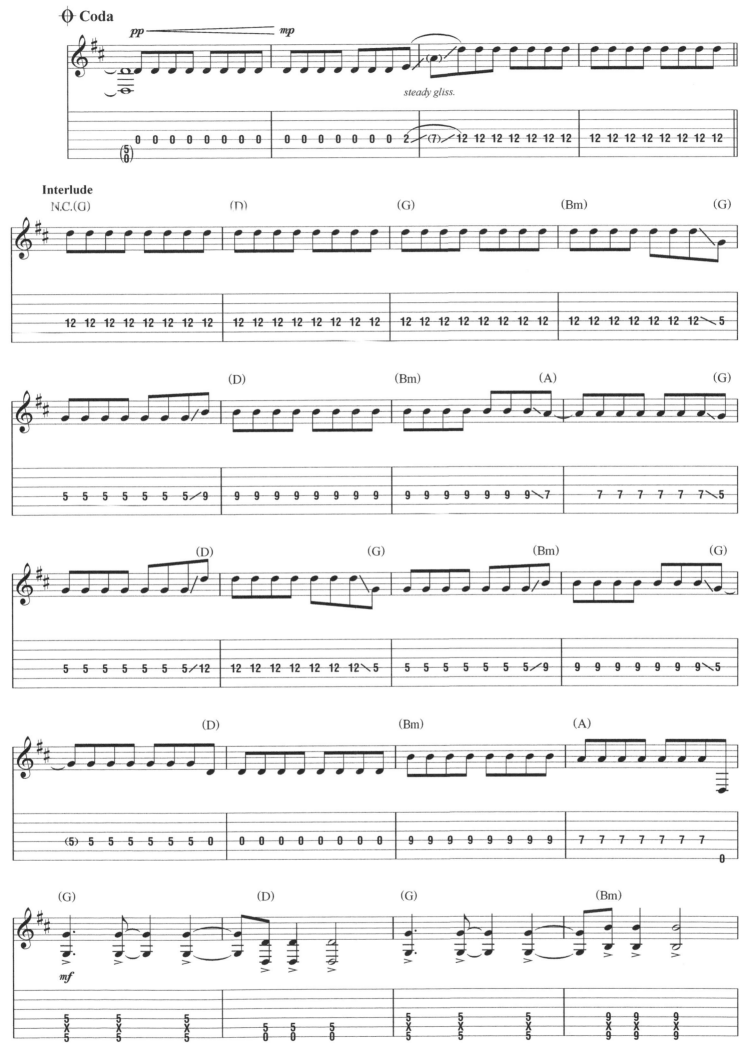

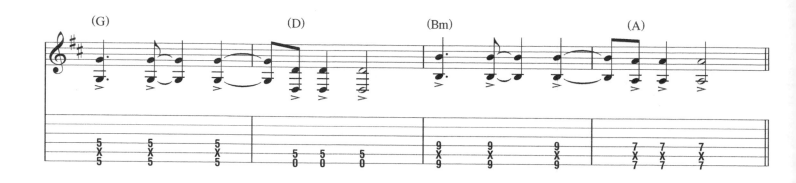

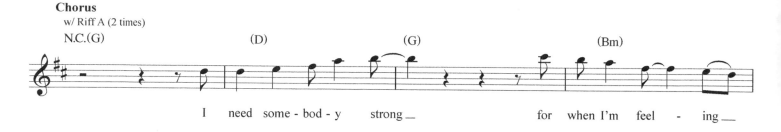

**Chorus**
w/ Riff A (2 times)

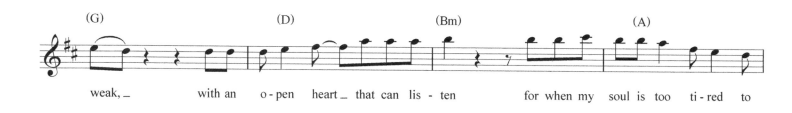

I need some-bod-y strong ___ for when I'm feel - ing ___

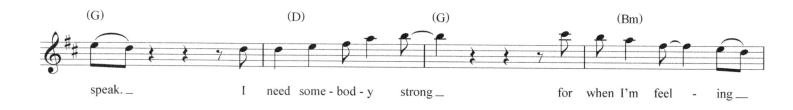

weak, ___ with an o - pen heart ___ that can lis - ten for when my soul is too ti - red to

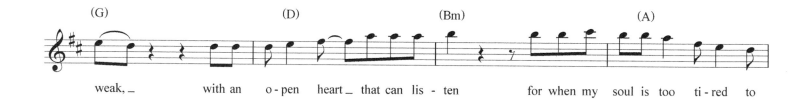

speak. ___ I need some-bod-y strong ___ for when I'm feel - ing ___

weak, ___ with an o - pen heart ___ that can lis - ten for when my soul is too ti - red to

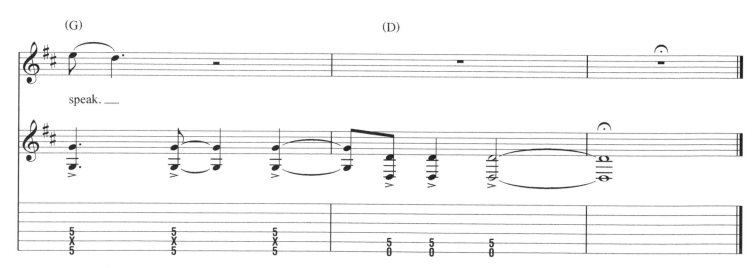

speak. ___

# I Belong To You

Words and Music by Brandi Carlile

Capo IV

*Recording sounds 2 steps higher than written due to capo.
Capoed fret is "0" in tab.

**Verse**

night I had___ the ex - act same dream as you.___ I

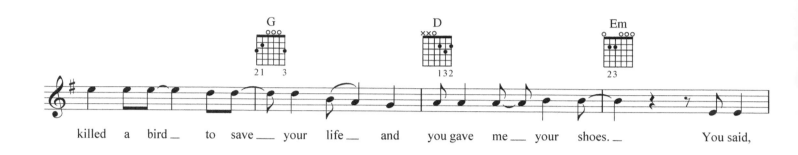

killed a bird___ to save___ your life___ and you gave me___ your shoes.___ You said,

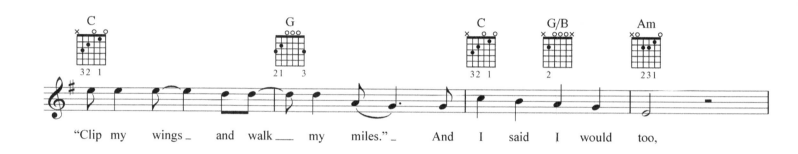

"Clip my wings___ and walk___ my miles."___ And I said I would too,

then I woke up but I was - n't gon - na___ tell you._____

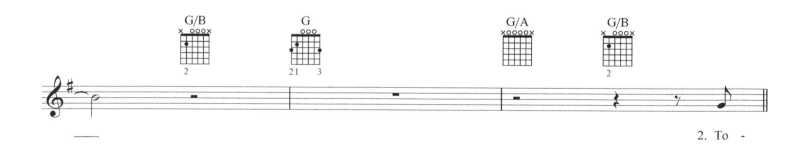

___ 2. To -

**Verse**

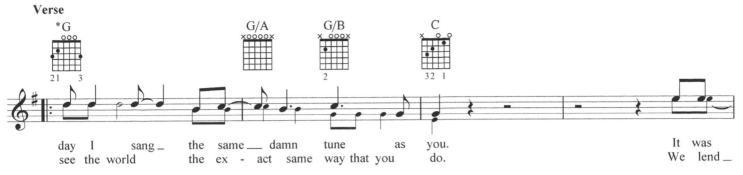

day I sang the same damn tune as you. It was

see the world the ex-act same way that you do. We lend

*2nd time, substitute Em chord.

"La-dy in Red," I hate that song, and I know you do too. You

our hands, and take our stands in tan-dem when we do. When I

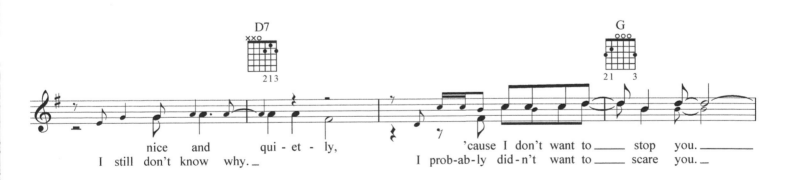

did-n't catch me sing-ing a-long but I al-ways sing with you

lied and said I knew the way, I hid my eyes from you.

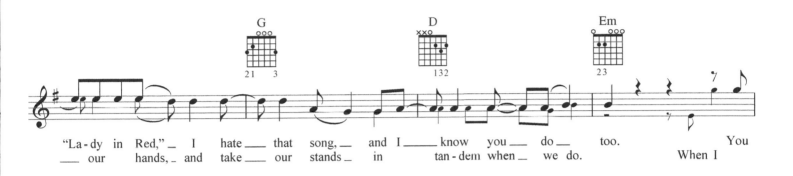

nice and qui-et-ly, 'cause I don't want to stop you.

I still don't know why. I prob-ab-ly did-n't want to scare you.

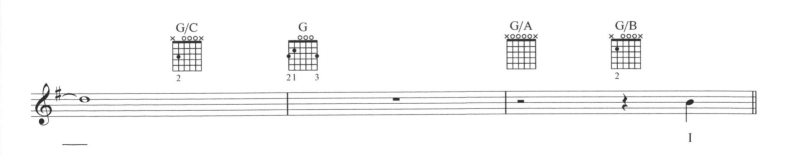

I

know    I    could _____    be    spend  -  ing    a    lit - tle    too _____

_____    much    time _____    with    you, _____    but

time    and    too _____    much _____    don't    be - long _____    to -

geth - er    like _____    we    do. _____    If

I    had _____    all _____    my    yes - ter - days _____    I'd    give    them    to _____

_____    you    too. _____    I    be - long _____ to

**Chorus**

you _____ now,        I be - long ___ to

you. _____        3. I

**Interlude**

**Verse**

3. I'm gon-na die ___ the ex - act same day as you. ___        On the

Gold-en Gate Bridge, _ I'll hold your hand ___ and howl at ___ the moon. ___

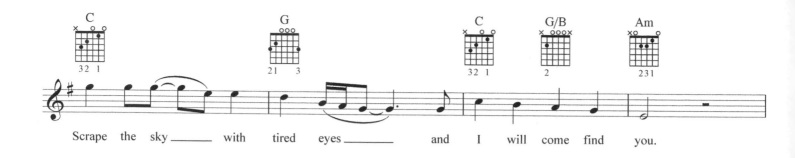

Scrape the sky _____ with tired eyes _____ and I will come find you.

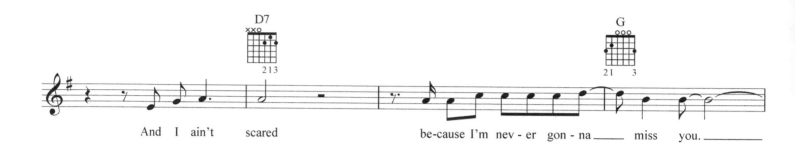

And I ain't scared be-cause I'm nev-er gon-na _____ miss you. _____

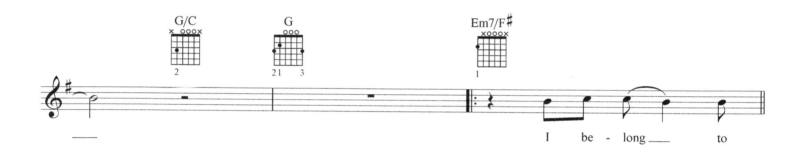

_____ I be - long _____ to

**Chorus**

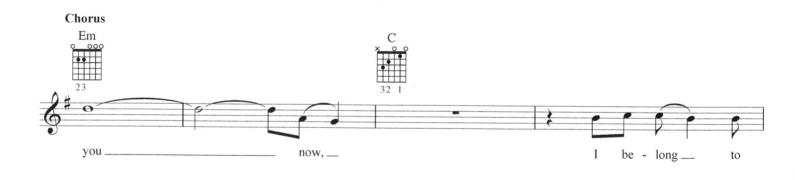

you _____ now, _____ I be - long _____ to

you _____

# Alibi

**Words and Music by Tim Hanseroth and Phil Hanseroth**

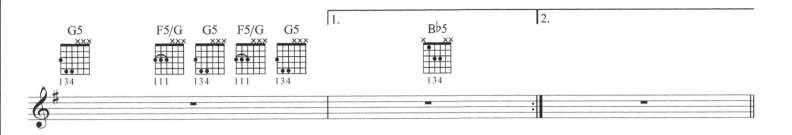

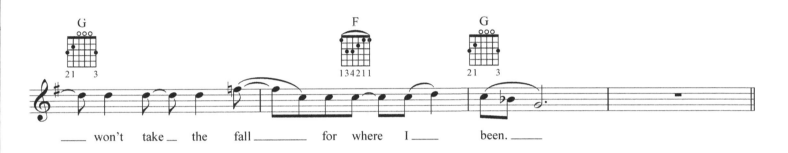

**Chorus**

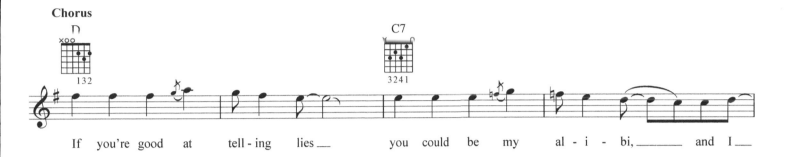

If you're good at tell-ing lies ___ you could be my al-i-bi, ___ and I ___

___ won't take ___ the fall ___ for where I ___ been. ___

**Interlude**

N.C.

**Verse**

w/ Riff A (2 times)

N.C.

3. I swear some ___ peo-ple in ___ this world, ___ they got ___ no ___ mor-al com-pass.

I know the wick-ed ones, ___ I feel ___ them ___ walk ___ a-mong us. The

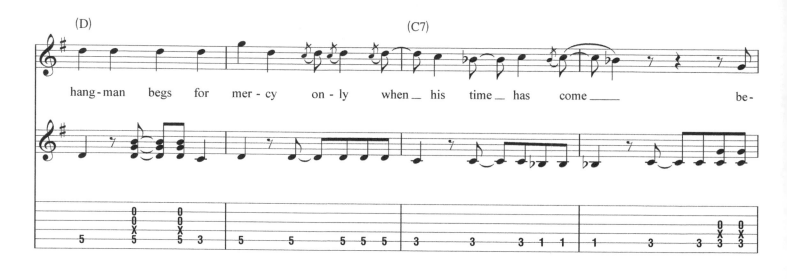

hang-man begs for mer-cy on-ly when __ his time __ has come _____ be-

*D.S. al Coda*

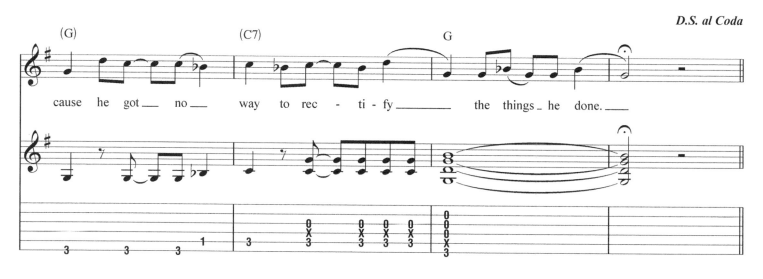

cause he got __ no __ way to rec - ti - fy _____ the things __ he done. ____

**Coda**

**Outro**

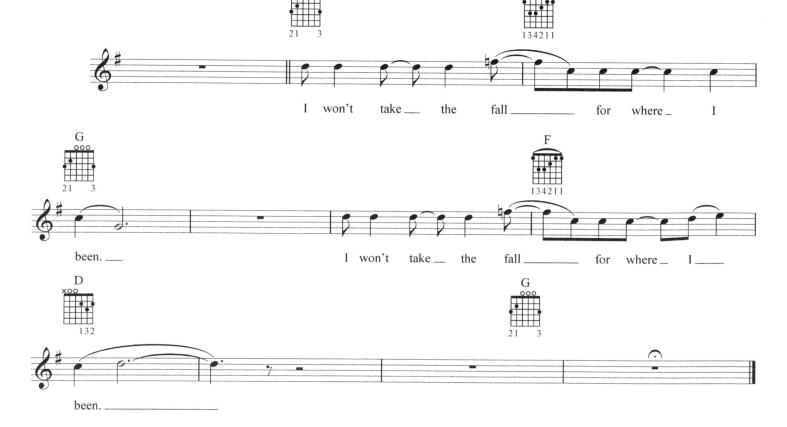

I won't take __ the fall _____ for where __ I

been. ____                    I won't take __ the fall _____ for where __ I ____

been. _____

# The Stranger At My Door

**Words and Music by Brandi Carlile**

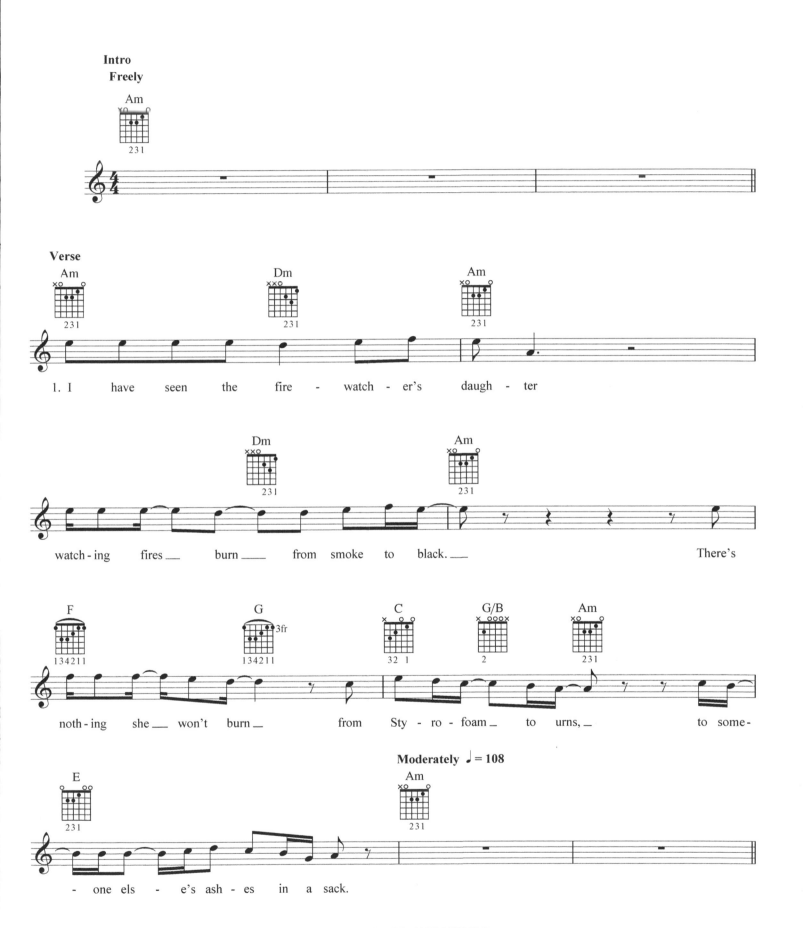

**Verse**

2. You can scorch \_\_ the met - al, you can e - ven melt \_\_ the glass. \_\_

You can pass \_\_ the time \_\_ here, \_\_ fire \_\_ lives in - to the past. \_\_ An

all - con - sum - ing flame that re - fines \_\_ and new be - gins. \_\_ It - 'll

take your fam - i - ly heir - looms, _____ but it can take your dark - est

sins. It's a

**Chorus**

good ol' bed - time sto - ry, give you night - mares \_\_ 'til you die, and the

ones that love \_\_ to tell it, hide \_\_\_\_ the mis - chief in \_\_ their eyes. \_\_ Con -

demn their sons to Ha - des and __ Ge - hen - na is full of guys, __ a - live and

*To Coda*

well, but there ain't no Hell for a fi - re - watch - er's daugh-

**Interlude**

- ter.

3. We ex -

**Verse**

- er - cise __ the de - mons of the things __ we used __ to know. __ The

gnash-ing of ___ the teeth ___ be - come ___ the rem - nants of our homes. ___ We

think we're mov - ing on, ___ from ma - te - ri - als ___ we long ___ to for - get ___

___ we ev - er sold ___ our ___ souls ___ to own. 4. There is a

**Verse**
**Freely**

chill - ing ab - so - lu - tion that we're giv - en at our birth, a

pow - er - ful ___ de - lu - sion, and a plague ___ up - on ___ the earth. ___ But

noth - ing scares me more than the stran - ger at ___ my door ___ who I fail ___

*rit.*

___ to give shel - ter, time, and worth.

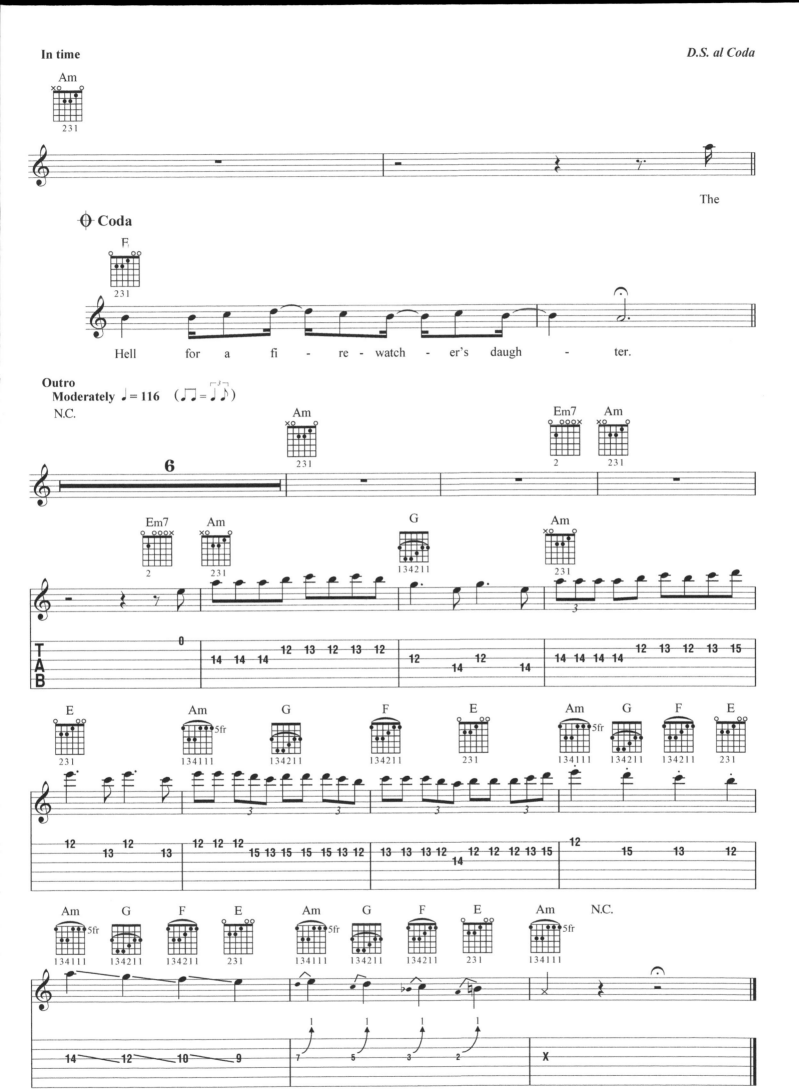

# Heroes And Songs

**Words and Music by Brandi Carlile**

thank yous and smiles and af - fec-tion for miles, _____ and I al-ways will look _ up to you. _

_____ You held o - pen the door ___ for who I'm sent here for ___ to come

**Chorus**

in and make my dreams _ come _ true. Al - though it was _ sad, ___ and it

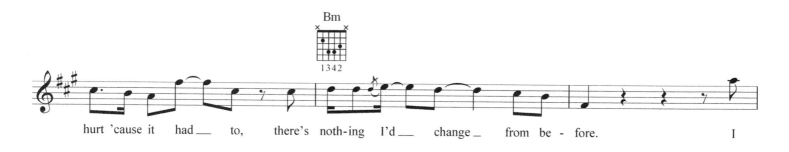

hurt 'cause it had ___ to, there's noth-ing I'd ___ change _ from be - fore. I

love you my friend, _ my _ dear means _ to an end, but you're not in my _ dreams _ an - y-more.

**Interlude**

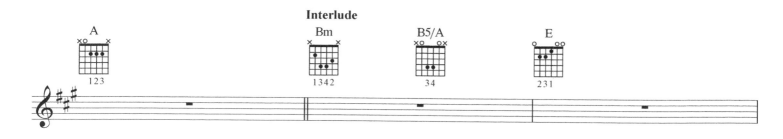

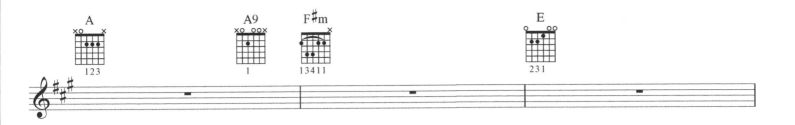

**Chorus**

Al - though it was — sad, —— and it hurt real - ly bad, — there's

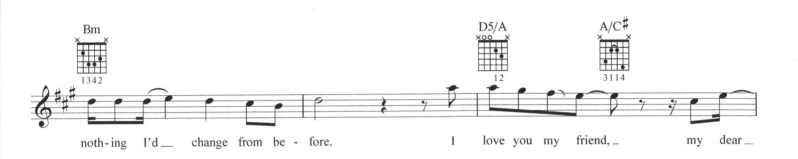

noth - ing I'd — change from be - fore. I love you my friend, — my dear —

— means — to an end, but you're not in my — dreams — an - y - more. —

You're not in my — dreams — an - y - more.

# Murder In The City

**Words and Music by Scott Avett and Timothy Avett**

No need to get o - ver - a - larmed. _____

I'm com - in' home.

I'm __ com - in' home. _

2. I won - der which of us is bet - ter, which one our par - ents loved _ the most.

I sure did get __ in lots __ of trou - ble,

and they seemed to let __ the oth - er go. A tear fell from my fa - ther's eyes. _

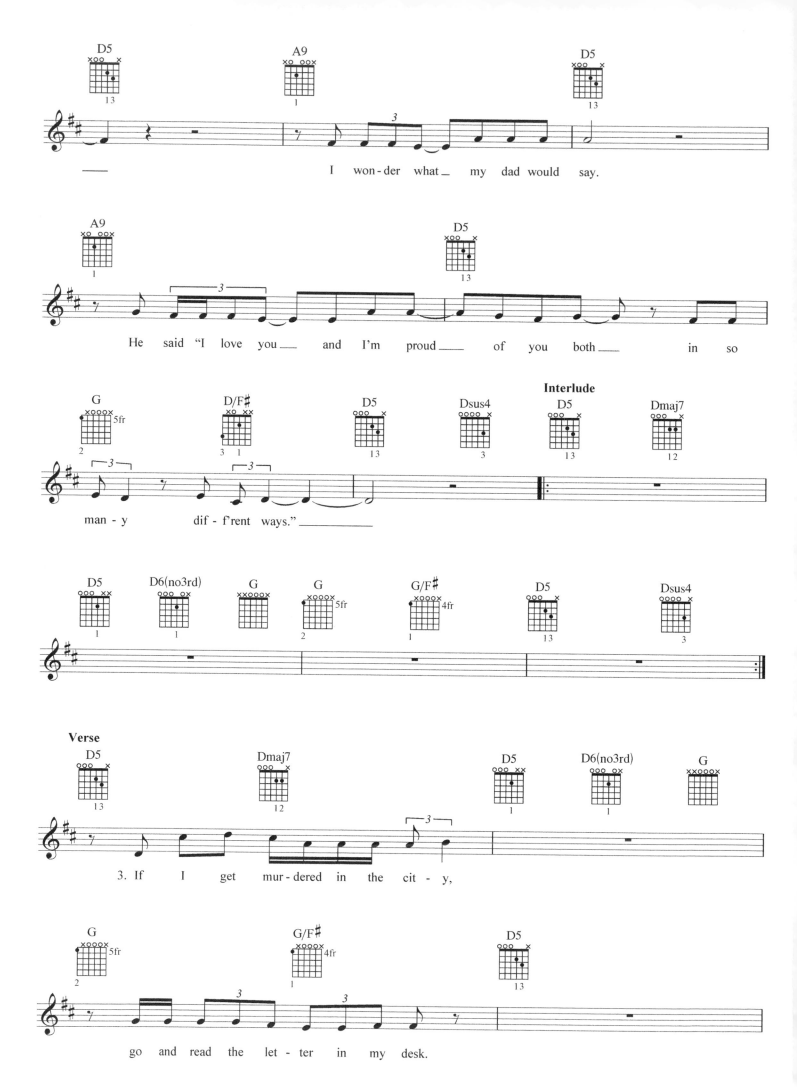

I won-der what\_ my dad would say.

He said "I love you \_\_\_ and I'm proud \_\_\_ of you both \_\_\_ in so

**Interlude**

man - y dif - f'rent ways." \_\_\_\_\_

**Verse**

3. If I get mur-dered in the cit - y,

go and read the let-ter in my desk.

# GUITAR NOTATION LEGEND

Guitar music can be notated three different ways: on a *musical staff*, in *tablature*, and in *rhythm slashes*.

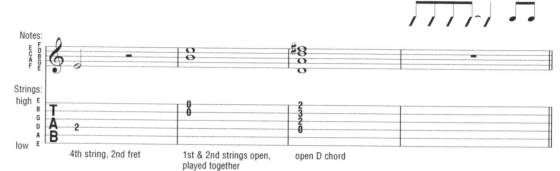

**RHYTHM SLASHES** are written above the staff. Strum chords in the rhythm indicated. Use the chord diagrams found at the top of the first page of the transcription for the appropriate chord voicings. Round noteheads indicate single notes.

**THE MUSICAL STAFF** shows pitches and rhythms and is divided by bar lines into measures. Pitches are named after the first seven letters of the alphabet.

**TABLATURE** graphically represents the guitar fingerboard. Each horizontal line represents a string, and each number represents a fret.

4th string, 2nd fret     1st & 2nd strings open, played together     open D chord

**HALF-STEP BEND:** Strike the note and bend up 1/2 step.

**WHOLE-STEP BEND:** Strike the note and bend up one step.

**GRACE NOTE BEND:** Strike the note and immediately bend up as indicated.

**SLIGHT (MICROTONE) BEND:** Strike the note and bend up 1/4 step.

**BEND AND RELEASE:** Strike the note and bend up as indicated, then release back to the original note. Only the first note is struck.

**PRE-BEND:** Bend the note as indicated, then strike it.

**VIBRATO:** The string is vibrated by rapidly bending and releasing the note with the fretting hand.

**WIDE VIBRATO:** The pitch is varied to a greater degree by vibrating with the fretting hand.

**HAMMER-ON:** Strike the first (lower) note with one finger, then sound the higher note (on the same string) with another finger by fretting it without picking.

**PULL-OFF:** Place both fingers on the notes to be sounded. Strike the first note and without picking, pull the finger off to sound the second (lower) note.

**LEGATO SLIDE:** Strike the first note and then slide the same fret-hand finger up or down to the second note. The second note is not struck.

**SHIFT SLIDE:** Same as legato slide, except the second note is struck.

**TRILL:** Very rapidly alternate between the notes indicated by continuously hammering on and pulling off.

**TAPPING:** Hammer ("tap") the fret indicated with the pick-hand index or middle finger and pull off to the note fretted by the fret hand.

**NATURAL HARMONIC:** Strike the note while the fret-hand lightly touches the string directly over the fret indicated.

**PINCH HARMONIC:** The note is fretted normally and a harmonic is produced by adding the edge of the thumb or the tip of the index finger of the pick hand to the normal pick attack.

**PICK SCRAPE:** The edge of the pick is rubbed down (or up) the string, producing a scratchy sound.

**MUFFLED STRINGS:** A percussive sound is produced by laying the fret hand across the string(s) without depressing, and striking them with the pick hand.

**PALM MUTING:** The note is partially muted by the pick hand lightly touching the string(s) just before the bridge.

**RAKE:** Drag the pick across the strings indicated with a single motion.

**TREMOLO PICKING:** The note is picked as rapidly and continuously as possible.

**VIBRATO BAR DIVE AND RETURN:** The pitch of the note or chord is dropped a specified number of steps (in rhythm), then returned to the original pitch.

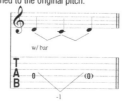

**VIBRATO BAR SCOOP:** Depress the bar just before striking the note, then quickly release the bar.

**VIBRATO BAR DIP:** Strike the note and then immediately drop a specified number of steps, then release back to the original pitch.

# EASY GUITAR WITH NOTES & TAB

*This series features simplified arrangements with notes, tab, chord charts, and strum and pick patterns.*

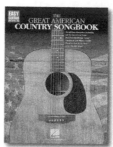  

## MIXED FOLIOS

| | | |
|---|---|---|
| 00702287 | Acoustic | $19.99 |
| 00702002 | Acoustic Rock Hits for Easy Guitar | $15.99 |
| 00702166 | All-Time Best Guitar Collection | $19.99 |
| 00702232 | Best Acoustic Songs for Easy Guitar | $16.99 |
| 00119835 | Best Children's Songs | $16.99 |
| 00703055 | The Big Book of Nursery Rhymes & Children's Songs | $16.99 |
| 00698978 | Big Christmas Collection | $19.99 |
| 00702394 | Bluegrass Songs for Easy Guitar | $15.99 |
| 00289632 | Bohemian Rhapsody | $19.99 |
| 00703387 | Celtic Classics | $16.99 |
| 00224808 | Chart Hits of 2016-2017 | $14.99 |
| 00267383 | Chart Hits of 2017-2018 | $14.99 |
| 00334293 | Chart Hits of 2019-2020 | $16.99 |
| 00403479 | Chart Hits of 2021-2022 | $16.99 |
| 00702149 | Children's Christian Songbook | $9.99 |
| 00702028 | Christmas Classics | $8.99 |
| 00101779 | Christmas Guitar | $14.99 |
| 00702141 | Classic Rock | $8.95 |
| 00159642 | Classical Melodies | $12.99 |
| 00253933 | Disney/Pixar's Coco | $16.99 |
| 00702203 | CMT's 100 Greatest Country Songs | $34.99 |
| 00702283 | The Contemporary Christian Collection | $16.99 |

| | | |
|---|---|---|
| 00196954 | Contemporary Disney | $19.99 |
| 00702239 | Country Classics for Easy Guitar | $24.99 |
| 00702257 | Easy Acoustic Guitar Songs | $17.99 |
| 00702041 | Favorite Hymns for Easy Guitar | $12.99 |
| 00222701 | Folk Pop Songs | $17.99 |
| 00126894 | Frozen | $14.99 |
| 00333922 | Frozen 2 | $14.99 |
| 00702286 | Glee | $16.99 |
| 00702160 | The Great American Country Songbook | $19.99 |
| 00702148 | Great American Gospel for Guitar | $14.99 |
| 00702050 | Great Classical Themes for Easy Guitar | $9.99 |
| 00275088 | The Greatest Showman | $17.99 |
| 00148030 | Halloween Guitar Songs | $14.99 |
| 00702273 | Irish Songs | $14.99 |
| 00192503 | Jazz Classics for Easy Guitar | $16.99 |
| 00702275 | Jazz Favorites for Easy Guitar | $17.99 |
| 00702274 | Jazz Standards for Easy Guitar | $19.99 |
| 00702162 | Jumbo Easy Guitar Songbook | $24.99 |
| 00232285 | La La Land | $16.99 |
| 00702258 | Legends of Rock | $14.99 |
| 00702189 | MTV's 100 Greatest Pop Songs | $34.99 |
| 00702272 | 1950s Rock | $16.99 |
| 00702271 | 1960s Rock | $16.99 |
| 00702270 | 1970s Rock | $24.99 |
| 00702269 | 1980s Rock | $16.99 |

| | | |
|---|---|---|
| 00702268 | 1990s Rock | $24.99 |
| 00369043 | Rock Songs for Kids | $14.99 |
| 00109725 | Once | $14.99 |
| 00702187 | Selections from O Brother Where Art Thou? | $19.99 |
| 00702178 | 100 Songs for Kids | $16.99 |
| 00702515 | Pirates of the Caribbean | $17.99 |
| 00702125 | Praise and Worship for Guitar | $14.99 |
| 00287930 | Songs from *A Star Is Born, The Greatest Showman, La La Land*, and More Movie Musicals | $16.99 |
| 00702285 | Southern Rock Hits | $12.99 |
| 00156420 | Star Wars Music | $16.99 |
| 00121535 | 30 Easy Celtic Guitar Solos | $16.99 |
| 00244654 | Top Hits of 2017 | $14.99 |
| 00283786 | Top Hits of 2018 | $14.99 |
| 00302269 | Top Hits of 2019 | $14.99 |
| 00355779 | Top Hits of 2020 | $14.99 |
| 00374083 | Top Hits of 2021 | $16.99 |
| 00702294 | Top Worship Hits | $17.99 |
| 00702255 | VH1's 100 Greatest Hard Rock Songs | $34.99 |
| 00702175 | VH1's 100 Greatest Songs of Rock and Roll | $34.99 |
| 00702253 | Wicked | $12.99 |

## ARTIST COLLECTIONS

| | | |
|---|---|---|
| 00702267 | AC/DC for Easy Guitar | $16.99 |
| 00156221 | Adele – 25 | $16.99 |
| 00396889 | Adele – 30 | $19.99 |
| 00702040 | Best of the Allman Brothers | $16.99 |
| 00702865 | J.S. Bach for Easy Guitar | $15.99 |
| 00702169 | Best of The Beach Boys | $16.99 |
| 00702292 | The Beatles — 1 | $22.99 |
| 00125796 | Best of Chuck Berry | $16.99 |
| 00702201 | The Essential Black Sabbath | $15.99 |
| 00702250 | blink-182 — Greatest Hits | $17.99 |
| 02501615 | Zac Brown Band — The Foundation | $17.99 |
| 02501621 | Zac Brown Band — You Get What You Give | $16.99 |
| 00702043 | Best of Johnny Cash | $17.99 |
| 00702090 | Eric Clapton's Best | $16.99 |
| 00702086 | Eric Clapton — from the Album Unplugged | $17.99 |
| 00702202 | The Essential Eric Clapton | $17.99 |
| 00702053 | Best of Patsy Cline | $17.99 |
| 00222697 | Very Best of Coldplay – 2nd Edition | $17.99 |
| 00702229 | The Very Best of Creedence Clearwater Revival | $16.99 |
| 00702145 | Best of Jim Croce | $16.99 |
| 00702278 | Crosby, Stills & Nash | $12.99 |
| 14042809 | Bob Dylan | $15.99 |
| 00702276 | Fleetwood Mac — Easy Guitar Collection | $17.99 |
| 00139462 | The Very Best of Grateful Dead | $16.99 |
| 00702136 | Best of Merle Haggard | $16.99 |
| 00702227 | Jimi Hendrix — Smash Hits | $19.99 |
| 00702288 | Best of Hillsong United | $12.99 |
| 00702236 | Best of Antonio Carlos Jobim | $15.99 |

| | | |
|---|---|---|
| 00702245 | Elton John — Greatest Hits 1970–2002 | $19.99 |
| 00129855 | Jack Johnson | $17.99 |
| 00702204 | Robert Johnson | $16.99 |
| 00702234 | Selections from Toby Keith — 35 Biggest Hits | $12.95 |
| 00702003 | Kiss | $16.99 |
| 00702216 | Lynyrd Skynyrd | $17.99 |
| 00702182 | The Essential Bob Marley | $16.99 |
| 00146081 | Maroon 5 | $14.99 |
| 00121925 | Bruno Mars – Unorthodox Jukebox | $12.99 |
| 00702248 | Paul McCartney — All the Best | $14.99 |
| 00125484 | The Best of MercyMe | $12.99 |
| 00702209 | Steve Miller Band — Young Hearts (Greatest Hits) | $12.95 |
| 00124167 | Jason Mraz | $15.99 |
| 00702096 | Best of Nirvana | $16.99 |
| 00702211 | The Offspring — Greatest Hits | $17.99 |
| 00138026 | One Direction | $17.99 |
| 00702030 | Best of Roy Orbison | $17.99 |
| 00702144 | Best of Ozzy Osbourne | $14.99 |
| 00702279 | Tom Petty | $17.99 |
| 00102911 | Pink Floyd | $17.99 |
| 00702139 | Elvis Country Favorites | $19.99 |
| 00702293 | The Very Best of Prince | $19.99 |
| 00699415 | Best of Queen for Guitar | $16.99 |
| 00109279 | Best of R.E.M. | $14.99 |
| 00702208 | Red Hot Chili Peppers — Greatest Hits | $17.99 |
| 00198960 | The Rolling Stones | $17.99 |
| 00174793 | The Very Best of Santana | $16.99 |
| 00702196 | Best of Bob Seger | $16.99 |
| 00146046 | Ed Sheeran | $17.99 |

| | | |
|---|---|---|
| 00702252 | Frank Sinatra — Nothing But the Best | $12.99 |
| 00702010 | Best of Rod Stewart | $17.99 |
| 00702049 | Best of George Strait | $17.99 |
| 00702259 | Taylor Swift for Easy Guitar | $15.99 |
| 00359800 | Taylor Swift – Easy Guitar Anthology | $24.99 |
| 00702260 | Taylor Swift — Fearless | $14.99 |
| 00139727 | Taylor Swift — 1989 | $19.99 |
| 00115960 | Taylor Swift — Red | $16.99 |
| 00253667 | Taylor Swift — Reputation | $17.99 |
| 00702290 | Taylor Swift — Speak Now | $16.99 |
| 00232849 | Chris Tomlin Collection – 2nd Edition | $14.99 |
| 00702226 | Chris Tomlin — See the Morning | $12.95 |
| 00148643 | Train | $14.99 |
| 00702427 | U2 — 18 Singles | $19.99 |
| 00702108 | Best of Stevie Ray Vaughan | $17.99 |
| 00279005 | The Who | $14.99 |
| 00702123 | Best of Hank Williams | $15.99 |
| 00194548 | Best of John Williams | $14.99 |
| 00702228 | Neil Young — Greatest Hits | $17.99 |
| 00119133 | Neil Young — Harvest | $14.99 |

Prices, contents and availability subject to change without notice.

Visit Hal Leonard online at **halleonard.com**

**STRUM & SING**

The Strum & Sing series for guitar and ukulele provides an unplugged and pared-down approach to your favorite songs — just the chords and the lyrics, with nothing fancy. These easy-to-play arrangements are designed for both aspiring and professional musicians.

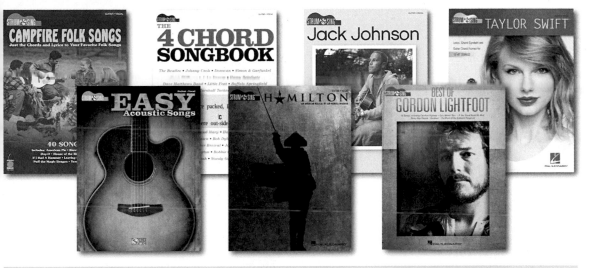

## GUITAR

| | | |
|---|---|---|
| **Acoustic Classics**<br>00191891 .......... $15.99 | **Easy Acoustic Songs**<br>00125478 .......... $19.99 | **Tom Petty –**<br>**Wildflowers & All the Rest**<br>00362682 .......... $14.99 |
| **Adele**<br>00159855 .......... $12.99 | **Billie Eilish**<br>00363094 .......... $14.99 | **Elvis Presley**<br>00198890 .......... $12.99 |
| **Sara Bareilles**<br>00102354 .......... $12.99 | **The Five-Chord Songbook**<br>02501718 .......... $14.99 | **Queen**<br>00218578 .......... $12.99 |
| **The Beatles**<br>00172234 .......... $17.99 | **Folk Rock Favorites**<br>02501669 .......... $14.99 | **Rock Around the Clock**<br>00103625 .......... $12.99 |
| **Blues**<br>00159335 .......... $12.99 | **Folk Songs**<br>02501482 .......... $14.99 | **Rock Ballads**<br>02500872 .......... $9.95 |
| **Zac Brown Band**<br>02501620 .......... $19.99 | **The Four-Chord Country Songbook**<br>00114936 .......... $15.99 | **Rocketman**<br>00300469 .......... $17.99 |
| **Colbie Caillat**<br>02501725 .......... $14.99 | **The Four Chord Songbook**<br>02501533 .......... $14.99 | **Ed Sheeran**<br>00152016 .......... $14.99 |
| **Campfire Folk Songs**<br>02500686 .......... $15.99 | **Four Chord Songs**<br>00249581 .......... $16.99 | **The Six-Chord Songbook**<br>02502277 .......... $17.99 |
| **Chart Hits of 2014-2015**<br>00142554 .......... $12.99 | **The Greatest Showman**<br>00278383 .......... $14.99 | **Chris Stapleton**<br>00362625 .......... $19.99 |
| **Chart Hits of 2015-2016**<br>00156248 .......... $12.99 | **Hamilton**<br>00217116 .......... $15.99 | **Cat Stevens**<br>00116827 .......... $17.99 |
| **Best of Kenny Chesney**<br>00142457 .......... $14.99 | **Jack Johnson**<br>02500858 .......... $19.99 | **Taylor Swift**<br>00159856 .......... $14.99 |
| **Christmas Carols**<br>00348351 .......... $14.99 | **Robert Johnson**<br>00191890 .......... $12.99 | **The Three-Chord Songbook**<br>00211634 .......... $12.99 |
| **Christmas Songs**<br>00171332 .......... $14.99 | **Carole King**<br>00115243 .......... $10.99 | **Top Christian Hits**<br>00156331 .......... $12.99 |
| **Kelly Clarkson**<br>00146384 .......... $14.99 | **Best of Gordon Lightfoot**<br>00139393 .......... $15.99 | **Top Hits of 2016**<br>00194288 .......... $12.99 |
| **Coffeehouse Songs for Guitar**<br>00285991 .......... $14.99 | **Dave Matthews Band**<br>02501078 .......... $10.95 | **Keith Urban**<br>00118558 .......... $14.99 |
| **Leonard Cohen**<br>00265489 .......... $14.99 | **John Mayer**<br>02501636 .......... $19.99 | **The Who**<br>00103667 .......... $12.99 |
| **Dear Evan Hansen**<br>00295108 .......... $16.99 | **The Most Requested Songs**<br>02501748 .......... $16.99 | **Yesterday**<br>00301629 .......... $14.99 |
| **John Denver Collection**<br>02500632 .......... $17.99 | **Jason Mraz**<br>02501452 .......... $14.99 | **Neil Young – Greatest Hits**<br>00138270 .......... $15.99 |
| **Disney**<br>00233900 .......... $17.99 | | |
| **Eagles**<br>00157994 .......... $14.99 | | |

## UKULELE

**The Beatles**
00233899 .......... $16.99

**Colbie Caillat**
02501731 .......... $10.99

**Coffeehouse Songs**
00138238 .......... $14.99

**John Denver**
02501694 .......... $17.99

**The 4-Chord Ukulele Songbook**
00114331 .......... $16.99

**Jack Johnson**
02501702 .......... $19.99

**John Mayer**
02501706 .......... $10.99

**The Most Requested Songs**
02501453 .......... $15.99

**Jason Mraz**
02501753 .......... $14.99

**Pop Songs for Kids**
00284415 .......... $16.99

**Sing-Along Songs**
02501710 .......... $16.99

**HAL•LEONARD®**

**halleonard.com**
Visit our website to see full song lists
or order from your favorite retailer.

# Get Better at Guitar

## ...with these Great Guitar Instruction Books from Hal Leonard!

### 101 GUITAR TIPS
**STUFF ALL THE PROS KNOW AND USE**
*by Adam St. James*

This book contains invaluable guidance on everything from scales and music theory to truss rod adjustments, proper recording studio set-ups, and much more.

00695737 Book/Online Audio ...............$17.99

### AMAZING PHRASING
*by Tom Kolb*

This book/audio pack explores all the main components necessary for crafting well-balanced rhythmic and melodic phrases. It also explains how these phrases are put together to form cohesive solos. The companion audio contains 89 demo tracks, most with full-band backing.

00695583 Book/Online Audio ...............$22.99

### ARPEGGIOS FOR THE MODERN GUITARIST
*by Tom Kolb*

Using this no-nonsense book with online audio, guitarists will learn to apply and execute all types of arpeggio forms using a variety of techniques, including alternate picking, sweep picking, tapping, string skipping, and legato.

00695862 Book/Online Audio ...............$22.99

### BLUES YOU CAN USE
*by John Ganapes*

This comprehensive source for learning blues guitar is designed to develop both your lead and rhythm playing. Includes: 21 complete solos • blues chords, progressions and riffs • turnarounds • movable scales and soloing techniques • string bending • utilizing the entire fingerboard • and more.

00142420 Book/Online Media..................$22.99

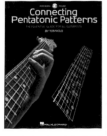

### CONNECTING PENTATONIC PATTERNS
*by Tom Kolb*

If you've been finding yourself trapped in the pentatonic box, this book is for you! This hands-on book with online audio offers examples for guitar players of all levels, from beginner to advanced. Study this book faithfully, and soon you'll be soloing all over the neck with the greatest of ease.

00696445 Book/Online Audio ...............$24.99

---

### FRETBOARD MASTERY
*by Troy Stetina*

Untangle the mysterious regions of the guitar fretboard and unlock your potential. This book familiarizes you with all the shapes you need to know by applying them in real musical examples, thereby reinforcing and reaffirming your newfound knowledge.

00695331 Book/Online Audio ...............$22.99

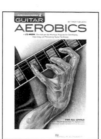

### GUITAR AEROBICS
*by Troy Nelson*

Here is a daily dose of guitar "vitamins" to keep your chops fine tuned! Musical styles include rock, blues, jazz, metal, country, and funk. Techniques taught include alternate picking, arpeggios, sweep picking, string skipping, legato, string bending, and rhythm guitar.

00695946 Book/Online Audio ...............$24.99

### GUITAR CLUES
**OPERATION PENTATONIC**
*by Greg Koch*

Whether you're new to improvising or have been doing it for a while, this book/audio pack will provide loads of delicious licks and tricks that you can use right away, from volume swells and chicken pickin' to intervallic and chordal ideas.

00695827 Book/Online Audio ...............$19.99

### PAT METHENY – GUITAR ETUDES

Over the years, in many master classes and workshops around the world, Pat has demonstrated the kind of daily workout he puts himself through. This book includes a collection of 14 guitar etudes he created to help you limber up, improve picking technique and build finger independence.

00696587..............................................$17.99

### PICTURE CHORD ENCYCLOPEDIA

This comprehensive guitar chord resource for all playing styles and levels features five voicings of 44 chord qualities for all twelve keys – 2,640 chords in all! For each, there is a clearly illustrated chord frame, as well as *an actual photo* of the chord being played!.

00695224..............................................$22.99

---

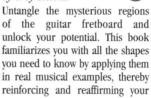

### RHYTHM GUITAR 365
*by Troy Nelson*

This book provides 365 exercises – one for every day of the year! – to keep your rhythm chops fine tuned. Topics covered include: chord theory; the fundamentals of rhythm; fingerpicking; strum patterns; diatonic and non-diatonic progressions; triads; major and minor keys; and more.

00103627 Book/Online Audio ...............$27.99

### SCALE CHORD RELATIONSHIPS
*by Michael Mueller & Jeff Schroedl*

This book/audio pack explains how to: recognize keys • analyze chord progressions • use the modes • play over nondiatonic harmony • use harmonic and melodic minor scales • use symmetrical scales • incorporate exotic scales • and much more!

00695563 Book/Online Audio ...............$17.99

### SPEED MECHANICS FOR LEAD GUITAR
*by Troy Stetina*

Take your playing to the stratosphere with this advanced lead book which will help you develop speed and precision in today's explosive playing styles. Learn the fastest ways to achieve speed and control, secrets to make your practice time really count, and how to open your ears and make your musical ideas more solid and tangible.

00699323 Book/Online Audio ...............$22.99

### TOTAL ROCK GUITAR
*by Troy Stetina*

This comprehensive source for learning rock guitar is designed to develop both lead and rhythm playing. It covers: getting a tone that rocks • open chords, power chords and barre chords • riffs, scales and licks • string bending, strumming, and harmonics • and more.

00695246 Book/Online Audio ...............$22.99

### *Guitar World Presents* STEVE VAI'S GUITAR WORKOUT

In this book, Steve Vai reveals his path to virtuoso enlightenment with two challenging guitar workouts — one 10-hour and one 30-hour — which include scale and chord exercises, ear training, sight-reading, music theory, and much more.

00119643..............................................$16.99

---